Explore Your Senses

TOUCH

by Laurence Pringle

BENCHMARK BOOKS

MARSHALL CAVENDISH
NEW YORK

The author wishes to thank Dr. Edward J. Kormondy, Chancellor and Professor of Biology (retired), University of Hawaii-Hilo/West Oahu for his careful reading of this text and his thoughtful and useful comments. The text has been improved by Dr. Kormondy's notes, however the author assumes full responsibility for the substance of the work, including any errors that may appear.

Benchmark Books
Marshall Cavendish Corporation
99 White Plains Road
Tarrytown, NY 10591

Library of Congress Cataloging-in-Publication Data
Pringle, Laurence P.
Touch / by Laurence Pringle.
p.   cm. — (Explore your senses)
Included bibliographical references and index.
Summary: Describes the sense of touch, how it works, and why it is important, discussing such related phenomena as goose bumps and phantom limbs, and examining this sense in a variety of other animals.
ISBN 0-7614-0738-3
1. Touch—Juvenile literature. [1. Touch. 2. Senses and sensation.] I. Title.
II. Series: Pringle, Laurence P.   Explore your senses.
QP451.P75   1999   612.8'8—dc21   98-28048   CIP   AC

Printed in Hong Kong

6   5   4   3   2   1

Photo research by Linda Sykes Picture Research, Hilton Head, SC

Cover photo: Photo Edit / Myrleen Ferguson
Picture credits: The photographs in this book are used by permission and through the courtesy of: Photo Edit:19 Prettyman; 11 David Young-Wolff. Photo Researchers: 12 Hans Reinhard/Okapia; 13 S. Nagendra; 16; 17 (right); 21 Jery Wachter; 23 Mark Newman; 25 Southern Illinois University; 27 (bottom left) David and Hayes Norris; 27 (bottom right) Tom Mc Hugh; 27 (top right) Will and Demi Mc Intyre; 28 Judy Mc Duffy; 29 (left) Leonard Lee Rue; 29 (right) Michael Mc Coy. Stock Boston: 8 William Johnson; 14 Stock Boston. The Image Bank: 4 Yellow Dog Productions; 4-5 (bottom) Steve Niedorf; 5 (right) LD Gordon; 9 Terje Rakke; 17 (left) Steve Dunwell.

Contents

Your sense of touch is unusual in many ways. One is its location. All of your other senses are limited to special small organs in your head: your sense of sight in your eyes, your sense of smell in your nose, your sense of taste in your mouth, and your senses of hearing and balance in your ears.

In contrast, your sense of touch is everywhere, from your head to your toes and everywhere in between. Your skin is one giant sense organ. It is by far the largest sense organ you have.

What we call the sense of touch involves more than touch. Your skin is also sensitive to pain, heat, cold, and pressure. Altogether, these skin senses protect you from harm. They are a vital defense against injury from a sharp stick, a hot plate, and other hurtful things.

As valuable as this defense is, the sense of touch is important in many other ways. Think of all the information you get from your sense of touch. With your eyes tightly closed you can feel a breeze and tell from which direction it is coming. You can touch all sorts of objects and identify them by feeling their shape and texture.

Think of all the pleasure you get from your sense of touch—from hugging a friend to petting a cat or dog. Both young pets and human infants need touching in order to develop normally.
Imagine not having a sense of touch! Life would be

Without a sense of touch we would have trouble picking up a ball. It is also vital for humans to be able to touch, to stroke the fur of a pet, and to feel a hug.

Your Sense of Touch

much less pleasant. It would also be difficult and even dangerous. We take our sense of touch for granted, but it is as important as sight, hearing, or any of the other human senses.

Your skin has many jobs. One of the most important is being a sense organ. It is much larger than any other sense organ. The skin of an adult weighs almost 9 pounds (4 kilograms) and covers about 20 square feet (2 square meters) in area.

This giant sense organ contains millions of *receptor* cells that are sensitive to touch, pain, and other *stimuli*. You can't see them. They can only be seen with a microscope. Even if you could look very closely at your skin you could not see them because they lie beneath the top layer of your skin.

This top layer is called the *epidermis*, which means "over skin." The thickness of the epidermis varies from place to place on your body. The epidermis of the skin of your eyelids may be only one-hundredth of an inch thick. On the bottoms of your feet, however, it is often a tenth of an inch (a quarter of a centimeter) or more thick.

The epidermis is divided into two layers. The top layer—the one you actually see and touch—is made up of tough flat cells that are dead. Bits of this upper epidermis are continually being shed. When you wash off dirt in the shower or bathtub, you also wash away dead cells from your epidermis. They are replaced by new cells that grow in the lower layer of the epidermis.

Your sense of touch, and other skin senses, are located below the epidermis, in the *dermis*. This deep part of the skin also contains blood vessels, hair roots, and *sweat glands*. These glands bring water from inside your body to the surface of your skin. They help keep your body from overheating.

Different Senses in Your Skin

Different kinds of touch receptors are located at different levels in the dermis. Receptors that detect pain are close to the surface. So are some cold receptors. The receptors that detect a light touch are close to the surface, while other touch receptors lie deeper in the dermis.

All of these receptors are connected by a chain of nerves to the brain. When you put one of your hands into cold water, the cold and the wetness is detected by skin receptor cells. A message is sent to your *spinal cord*, then up to your brain. Cells in the brain can figure out where the message is coming from. Your brain tells you, "My right hand feels wet and cold."

In this way, the sense of touch is like vision, hearing, and other senses. Just as seeing occurs in your brain, not your eyes, what you feel on your skin is actually felt in your brain.

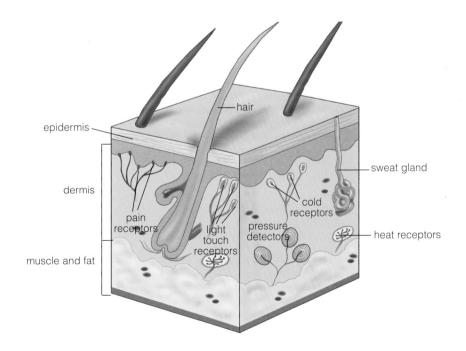

Look at your hands. Try to imagine life without your sense of touch. You would have to rely on your eyesight to tell whether you were touching something. You would have to look to see whether you were holding a pen correctly, putting a button in a buttonhole, or turning the page of a book. Many things you do easily each day—at work or play—would become difficult tasks.

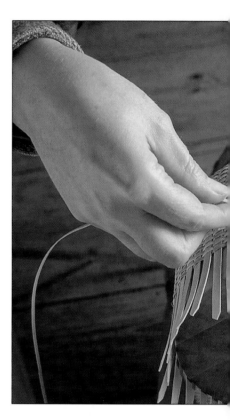

Thanks to your sense of touch, your hands have an amazing ability to perform tasks and give you vital information. Watch the hands of a pianist as they dance across the keys of a piano, sometimes striking a dozen or more notes in a few seconds. Your own fingers may fly as you push the control buttons of a video game.

In some science museums, visitors can try to find their way through a maze in total darkness. Within the maze there are twists and turns, floors that tilt up or down, narrow spaces and bigger ones. Your sense of hearing helps a bit, but you are surrounded by pitch blackness, so you rely almost entirely on your sense of touch.

These mazes can be scary. Museum workers stand ready to help anyone who needs assistance. Most people find their way through the maze without help. However, after a few moments in the maze they realize just how vital their sense of touch is.

Life Without Touch

Both simple and complex tasks depend on the sense of touch in our fingers. Imagine tying a shoelace knot without feeling the laces!

Even though your whole skin is one giant sense organ, some parts of your body are more sensitive to touch than others. Touch receptors are scarce in some places and plentiful in others. The drawing on this page shows where touch receptors are clustered together. Some of the most sensitive places are your fingertips, your face, and the back of your neck.

When receptors in your skin sense a touch, or pressure, or cold, messages are sent to your spinal cord. The messages zoom quickly to a part of the brain called the *thalamus*, where they are sorted, then sent on to different parts of the brain's *somatosensory cortex*. In the cortex the messages reach special places that are assigned to different parts of your body. The somatosensory cortex contains the brain's map of your body. There's a nerve center for your left thumb, another for your right shoulder, and so on. This is where the touch or pain or other stimulus on your skin actually gets your attention.

Often you will notice that the receptors in your skin soon stop sending signals. Suppose you put on a wristwatch, or pull on a heavy sweatshirt. A first you feel the watch on your wrist; the weight of the sweatshirt is very noticeable. But after a few moments, you hardly notice either one.

This is a good thing. Being constantly reminded of every stimulus to our skin senses would be over-

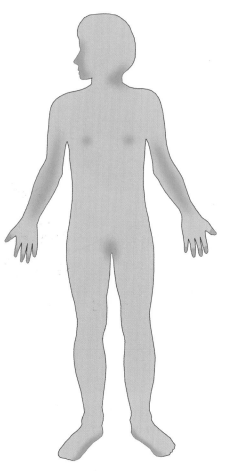

Touch receptors are most concentrated on your skin in the areas shown in color.

How Your Sense of Touch Works

whelming. While your sense of touch ignores certain kinds of information from your skin, it stays ready to respond to new information.

somatosensory cortex

thalamus (deep in brain)

You may feel the weight of a heavy sweatshirt when you first pull it on, but hardly notice it after a few moments.

Our sense of touch gives us vital information about our surroundings and about possible danger. It also helps satisfy a basic need, the need to be touched.

Touch tells a baby animal that it is safe. Scientists have found that baby rats, called pups, thrive and grow well when they are licked and nuzzled by their mother. Being touched causes the pups to produce a chemical called a *hormone* that stimulates their growth. When their mother is removed, the pups produce less hormone and their growth suffers. The scientists discovered that heavy stroking with a paintbrush caused the pups to grow normally. The brushing probably felt like the licking of their mother. The pups did best of all, however, when they were touched by their own mother.

Rats are *mammals*. All mammal mothers provide their newborn young with milk. As the young nurse they are in close contact with their mother. They get nourishing milk and are also nourished by being touched.

Mammals called *primates* do a lot of touching. Primates include gorillas, chimpanzees, all sorts of monkeys—and humans. At a zoo you may have seen a mother monkey holding its young close to its body as it leaped from branch to branch. You may have seen monkeys or other primates at the zoo sitting close together, grooming each other's fur. When

Rat pups do not grow well when they cannot touch, and be touched by, their mothers.

The Power of Touch

young monkeys do not have much contact with their mothers, they grow up to be poor mothers themselves.

All primates crave touch. Human infants and children also suffer harm when they are not cuddled and held by their parents. This need becomes especially clear with babies who are born before they are fully developed. These *premature* babies have to have special care in a hospital. For days and even weeks they cannot go home to be held and cuddled by their parents.

It is vital for premature babies to get plenty of touching. If a baby's parents cannot visit often, it can be given firm but gentle massages by nurses or hospital volunteers. Babies who are given this touching gain weight much faster than neglected infants. They are also more alert and active.

People never outgrow their need to be touched, and to touch others. This is one reason many people enjoy petting and stroking the fur of pet cats and dogs. And the power of touch affects people in surprising ways. One study showed that customers in restaurants who were touched on the hand or shoulder by their waitress gave bigger tips than customers who were not touched.

Monkeys do a lot of touching and often groom the fur of family members.

Touch receptors are tightly clustered on the tips of fingertips. You can even read with your eyes closed by running your fingers over letters that are raised above the paper surface. These are called embossed letters. Tracing the shapes of letters, you can spell out words.

Blind people use a better method of reading with their fingertips. This system is called Braille, after the man who created it. Louis Braille was born in France in 1809. At the age of three he was blinded in an accident. Still, he became a good student. While still a teenager he became a teacher at a school for the blind in Paris.

The students there had only a few books with big, embossed letters that they could read. Louis Braille tried to create a better way to help blind people read, without success. Then an army officer told him about "night writing." To avoid using lights at night, army units sometimes sent messages made up of coded marks punched into thick paper. In the dark, the message could be felt with fingertips.

Louis Braille began to experiment with this idea. After several years of trial and error, in 1829 he published his system of raised dots. It was a simple but effective way for blind people to read by running their fingers along patterns of raised dots. The Braille method was not an instant success. Sadly for Louis Braille, its value was not recognized until after

Blind people can read well by sensing the Braille patterns of raised dots with their fingertips.

Reading With Your Fingers

he died, in 1852. Now it is used all over the world.

Braille is more than an alphabet of twenty-six letters. It includes coded ways to show capital letters and numbers. Braille can also be used by musicians, to read music while playing. In fact, Braille makes the reading and writing of music easier for blind people than for those who can see. And blind people can also use devices to write in Braille.

Tests of blind students show that they can read Braille much faster than they can read embossed letters. They cannot read as fast as students who can see, but they can still read well. Some blind students read with both index fingers, one trailing the other over the dots. They are the fastest readers of Braille writing.

The Braille Alphabet

a	b	c	d	e	f	g	h	i	j
k	l	m	n	o	p	q	r	s	t
u	v	w	x	y	z				

When a mosquito lands delicately on your skin, you usually feel it. You also know when a leaf brushes lightly against your skin. Your sense of touch is very sensitive.

Pain receptors are not so sensitive. They have what is called a *threshold* of sensitivity. If you press the tines of a fork lightly against the skin of your arm, the stimulus does not reach the pain threshold. You feel the pressure of the sharp tines, but no pain. When you press the tines harder, the stimulus reaches the threshold of your pain receptors. Your skin begins to hurt.

Some people are more sensitive to pain than others. They have a lower pain threshold. Some have a high threshold for pain, and aren't bothered by bumps and scrapes that feel painful to others. In general, females seem to have higher pain thresholds than males.

Sometimes a person's pain receptors send messages to the brain that say "Ouch, that hurts!" but the brain says, "That's not important now." You may have had that experience. Perhaps you were hurt in a game of soccer or basketball. You wanted to keep playing and help your team win. You ignored the feeling of pain, or didn't even notice it until after the game.

The job of the pain receptors of your body is to warn you of possible harm. To do their job, they are

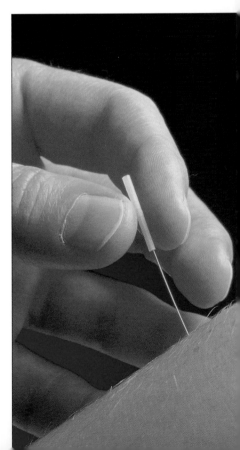

The fine needles used in acupuncture sometimes give people relief from pain or nausea.

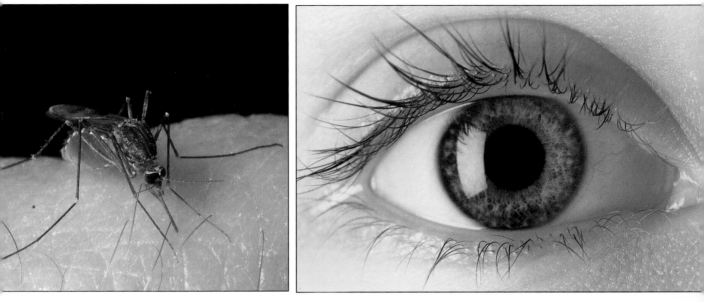

People usually feel the touch of a mosquito landing on their skin. The many pain receptors on the surface of eyes help protect them from harm.

concentrated in some places and scarce in others. There are few pain receptors inside our bodies. When a person's heart or other organ hurts, the pain is usually felt elsewhere. Doctors call this *referred* pain. A person having a heart attack may feel referred pain in the skin over the heart and also along the left arm and shoulder. Pain in a person's liver may be felt on the right side of the neck.

Many pain receptors are clustered on the surface of your eye because even a tiny speck of dirt can damage your sense of sight. Fewer pain receptors are found on your feet and hands. We rely so much on our hands to give us important information from our sense of touch that it would be a disadvantage to have fingers that were very sensitive to pain.

The sense of touch has much more to do with the brain than with receptors on your fingertips. What you feel—touch, heat, pain, and so on— occurs in your brain.

What happens in the brain is still being studied by scientists. One puzzle about how people feel pain is the mystery of *phantom limbs*.

Sometimes, after a serious injury or infection, part of a person's leg or arm is removed, or amputated. The limb is gone. All of the sense receptors in the amputated limb are gone. Nevertheless, the person still feels that the limb is there.

Even if an arm was amputated, the person may feel that he or she is still moving the arm, hand, and fingers. The person can see there is no arm, yet feel things. As the person walks, the missing arm feels as if it is swinging normally at his or her side. The arm does not exist but it still may itch, or ache with a muscle cramp. That's why it is called a ghost or phantom limb.

Almost all people who have had a limb removed continue to feel it some of the time. Many suffer from pain. To help ease their suffering, scientists are trying to understand why phantom limbs occur.

The answer to the mystery probably lies in changes in the brain's sensory map of the body. Even though a person knows an arm is missing, nerve cells, or neurons, in his or her sensory map

Mystery of the Phantom Limbs

(in the somatosensory cortex) do not know it. The neurons that normally receive messages from that arm stay ready to receive them. However, when no more messages from the arm arrive, the brain begins to change its sensory map a bit.

This remapping allows messages from other body parts—the person's shoulder, for instance—to reach the neurons that await messages from the missing arm. Depending on the remapping that occurs in the brain, a person can be touched on the shoulder, cheek, or chest and feel the touch in his or her phantom limb. Other parts of the brain are involved in the touch senses. They, too, may help produce feelings from a phantom limb. However, the discovery that the brain's sensory map changes after an amputation is an important step toward solving the mystery of phantom limbs.

People sometimes feel pain or other sensations from a missing limb.

Within your body you have a kind of touch sense that enables you to keep track of the location of your legs, arms, head, and the rest of your body. Here's a way to test this sensory system: Close your eyes. Hold your two hands far apart. Make fists but leave your two thumbs pointing inward. Now, keeping your eyes closed, move your hands toward each other and touch the tips of your thumbs together.

Think about what you just did. Without looking, you were able quickly to move your thumbs exactly where you wanted them. Without looking, you know the position of your body and limbs. Receptors called *proprioceptors* make this possible. The word proprioceptor means "one's own receptor."

Most proprioceptors are located in your body's muscles, joints, and *tendons*, which hold muscles and bones together. They detect whether a muscle is relaxed or tight. In your brain, information from all of your body's proprioceptors gives you a mental picture of your body in its surroundings.

Your proprioceptors are always at work but are especially important when you are on the move. Walking may seem simple and easy, but it depends on the automatic teamwork by your brain, your sense of balance, and your proprioceptors. These sense receptors are even more vital when you dance, dive from a diving board, or try to dribble past a defender on the basketball court. Your mus-

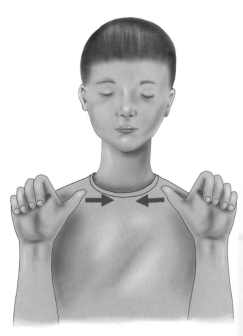

Can you touch your thumbs together without looking?

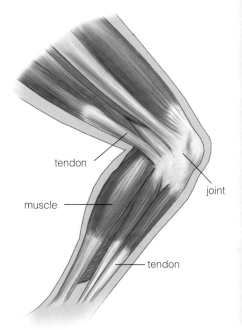

tendon

joint

muscle

tendon

Keeping Track of Your Body

cles make many split-second moves automatically, thanks to your proprioceptors.

As a gymnast performs, proprioceptors enable dozens of muscles to stretch or contract in a few seconds.

Extremely cold temperatures—below freezing—can cause cells and tissues to die. Long exposure to freezing temperatures can cause a person's body temperature to drop below 95 degrees Fahrenheit (35 degrees Celsius). This is a dangerous condition called *hypothermia*.

Extremely warm temperatures can damage skin and muscles. Inside the body, a high temperature—above 106 degrees Fahrenheit (41 degrees Celsius)—can harm the brain and other organs. This is called *hyperthermia*.

The skin is the body's vital defense against both heat and cold, so there are both heat and cold receptors in the dermis layer. The receptors that respond to cold temperatures are closest to the surface, just below the epidermis. They are the most abundant on the face. Heat receptors lie deeper in the dermis.

Just as hands have small numbers of pain receptors, they also have few temperature receptors. This enables us to keep using our hands and their vital sense of touch on a very cold day. Fingers are not as sensitive to cold or heat as some other body parts. This is why doctors say that touching your lips to a person's forehead to see if they feel feverish is a better guide than touching the forehead with your hand.

Sometimes your cold receptors can be fooled. If

Cold receptors lie close to the surface of the skin, and are most abundant on a person's face.

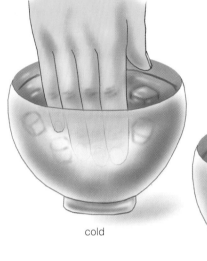

cold

warm

hot

you touch an ice cube or grab a big icicle with your bare hand, the ice may feel hot. This occurs because very cold temperatures stimulate both cold and pain receptors. The combination of stimuli may seem like a hot sensation.

When you jump into a swimming pool the water often seems shockingly cold. In a few moments, however, the water feels more comfortable. If someone asks you how the water is, you might say, "Great—once you get used to it." The water temperature has not changed, but the cold receptors in your skin have adapted to the temperature. They stop responding to the cold, but are ready to react if you swim into an area of colder water.

Hot and cold receptors can sometimes be tricked. Try this: Set three bowls of water close together, with cold water on the left, hot water on the right, and luke-warm water in the middle. Put your left hand in the hot water and your right hand in the cold water. Leave them for a minute or two. Then lift them out and put both hands in the lukewarm water. Does the lukewarm water feel the same on both hands?

When all the feathers are plucked from a dead chicken, duck, or goose, the bird's skin is covered with little raised bumps. These are the places where feathers once grew. Sometimes humans have this pebbly-looking skin. We call it goose flesh, goose pimples, or goose bumps.

Humans and other mammals have hair instead of feathers, and our goose bumps occur where hairs grow from our skin. About 100,000 hairs grow on our heads but these are only a small part of the total: five million hairs! Except for parts of our hands and feet, fine hairs grow almost everywhere on our skin, even on toes and elbows.

People get goose bumps mostly on their arms and legs. They appear when receptors in the skin suddenly detect cold air. This causes skin muscles to tighten. This may also cause the muscles to twitch, in a *shivering* movement. Shivering produces heat, and is a defense against cold. Goose bumps are also a defense against cold, as little muscles at the base of hairs cause the hairs to stand up. This helps to trap a layer of air against the skin, and keep colder air outside that layer.

Besides responding to cold, hairs respond to touch. The actual hairs you see on your head, arm, and so on are dead tissue. You can cut them without pain. Down in the dermis, however, each hair has a live root enclosed in its *follicle*. Both pain and touch

Each hair has a tiny muscle that causes it to stand up—a defense against cold air.

24

Goose Bumps and Hair Follicles

receptors lie near the base of the follicle.

If you pull the dead end of a hair, it stimulates the pain receptors at the hair's live end. And when you touch some of your hairs lightly, the movement of the hairs reaches the touch receptors at the base of those hairs.

The touch receptors near hair follicles are an important part of our skin senses. They are the very first receptors to detect a light touch or a breeze that causes the hairs to move.

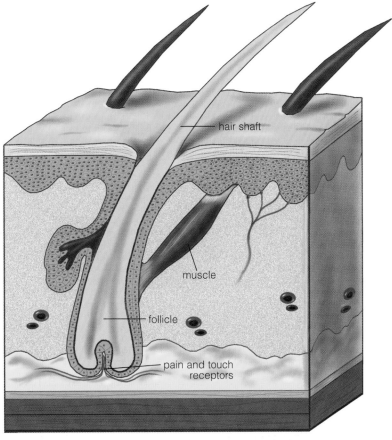

hair shaft

muscle

follicle

pain and touch receptors

A chilly wind may give you goose bumps. A scary sound can do the same, causing the little hairs on the back of your neck to rise. Hairs of other mammals, too, lift up when they are alarmed. You may have seen a cat with its back and tail hair raised. This makes the cat look bigger than normal, a defense against an enemy.

Cats of all kinds, including lions and tigers, have special hollow hairs that are extensions of their sense of touch. We call them whiskers, or *vibrissae*, which is the scientific name for these special thick hairs.

If you were asked to draw a cat's whiskers, you would mark several long vibrissae growing from both cheeks. These are the most noticeable whiskers, but cats also have vibrissae above their eyes, under their chin, on their upper lip, and on the elbows of their front legs. All of these whiskers are important to a cat's sense of touch.

Like human hairs, whiskers are connected to touch receptors in the skin. Like human hairs, whiskers extend the sense of touch beyond the skin. Since cat whiskers are long, they extend the sense of touch quite far. This is helpful for cats since they are often active at night. Even with good night vision, cats need their whiskers to find their way in the dark.

If you lightly touch the whiskers above a cat's eyes, the cat usually blinks. These vibrissae guard the cat's eyes and give the cat warning of a stick or other object coming from above.

A cat's eyebrow, cheek, and chin whiskers help it judge the size of an opening. When these whiskers brush against the sides of an entrance, the cat is warned that its body might not fit through. If

Whiskers at Work

a cat catches a mouse or other prey, the chin and cheek whiskers bend forward. They enclose the mouse and help the cat keep track of the mouse's movements.

Mice, rats, and other rodents also have whiskers that extend their sense of touch. The long cheek whiskers of rats actually vibrate in the air. The pattern of their vibration is changed when something touches them. This probably helps rats react quickly to whatever their whiskers touch.

Rats, other rodents, and cats are not the only animals that extend their sense of touch with whiskers. Seals and walruses have long whiskers that help them find food underwater where there is little light. And in some of the muddiest, murkiest ponds and rivers, catfish feel for food with several pairs of whiskers (also called barbels). Catfish can't see well, but they gobble down a worm or other prey if it touches one of their whiskers.

A rat's quivering whiskers help it sense its surroundings in the dark.

Cats and catfish learn about their surroundings from the touch receptors in their whiskers.

cientists studying the senses of cats have found more than a dozen different kinds of receptors in their skin. Cats have a more complicated system of skin senses than people. This is no surprise. Name any sense, and you can find some kinds of animals that outshine humans. A variety of creatures, from spiders to moles, have a more sensitive sense of touch than people. Some are adept at detecting faint vibrations.

Some female spiders make wheel-shaped webs, called orb webs, from silk their bodies produce. Once the web is complete, the spider waits in its center or at an edge. She keeps one foot on a key line in the web's design. When an insect flies or jumps into some of the web's sticky threads, the spider feels vibrations caused by its prey. It runs along the web's dry lines to capture a meal.

Burrowing underground are creatures whose whole bodies are strongly sensitive to touch. Moles have poor eyesight and spend most of their lives under the soil surface. Their snouts are covered with touch receptors. Vibrissae grow all over their bodies. They rely almost entirely on their sense of touch to find earthworms and other food.

Many kinds of fish have a touch sense that is far more sensitive than that of people—or even of moles. Receptors in the sides of their bodies detect vibrations in the water around them. The vibrations

A spider waits for vibrations caused by an insect stuck in a web's sticky threads.

are caused by other creatures moving in the water. This system helps fish locate food and avoid enemies.

In the tropics, some frogs are able to detect vibrations in mud or water. This warns them of approaching danger. Some frogs also send messages to others of their kind by causing vibrations. In Puerto Rico, male white-lipped frogs hit their throat sacs against the mud. This makes a thumping sound. The males also make chirping sounds. Both the chirps and the thumps are aimed at attracting a mate. In Malaysia, certain female tree frogs tap their toes to attract mates. Sending messages by causing ground vibrations is called *seismic communication*.

Animals are masters of the sense of touch. The touch sense of humans is less sensitive than that of moles and many other creatures. Nevertheless, we could not survive without the information and the nurturing we receive from the touch sense.

Moles find food underground with their sense of touch, while some tree frogs send messages by tapping or thumping the ground.

Braille—a system of raised dots representing letters and numbers that allows blind people to read by running their fingertips over the dots.

dermis—the deep part of the skin, below the surface epidermis. Nerve cells sensitive to touch, pain, heat, and cold lie in the dermis.

epidermis—the upper surface layer of the skin that protects the dermis layer. The epidermis is made up of a lower layer of live cells and an outermost layer of dead cells.

follicle—a tube that encloses a shaft of hair, including its living root, below the skin surface. The follicle is surrounded by nerve cells that are sensitive to pain and touch.

goose bumps—a pebbly skin surface that occurs when cold air causes muscles to contract and short hairs on the skin to stand up. Goose bumps are one of the body's defenses against cold.

hormones—chemicals produced in the body that affect the working of organs and the well-being of the body, including its growth.

hyperthermia—dangerous, unusually high temperature, when the body temperature rises above 106 degrees Fahrenheit (41 degrees Celsius).

hypothermia—dangerously low body temperature, 95 degrees Fahrenheit (35 degrees Celsius) or lower.

mammals—animals with backbones that nurse their young with milk.

phantom limb—an arm or leg that has been removed, yet continues to be felt as if it were still attached. People who have had a limb removed often feel pain and other sensations where the missing limb used to be.

premature baby—an infant born several weeks or more before the normal time of birth, which is after about nine months in the womb. Because they have not had the normal amount of time developing in their mother's body, premature babies usually need special care in order to survive.

primates—the order of mammals that includes monkeys, apes, and humans.

proprioceptors—receptors in muscles and tendons that enable the brain to be aware of the position of the head, limbs, and body.

receptors—nerve cells, or neurons, that are sensitive to touch, pain, or other stimuli, such as light and sound.

referred pain—pain that occurs in an internal organ, such as the heart, that is actually felt somewhere on the skin. In the case of a heart attack, the pain is often felt in the left arm and shoulder.

Glossary

seismic communication—communicating by sending and receiving vibrations through the soil. The word seismic come from a Greek work for "shake," and is usually applied to earthquakes.

shivering—an automatic response of the skin to cold that causes muscles to twitch. This produces heat and helps warm the skin surface.

somatosensory cortex—an area of the brain's cortex where pain and other stimuli to the skin are identified.

spinal cord—the part of the central nervous system that is enclosed by and protected by the vertebrae that make up the backbone. The spinal cord is connected directly to the brain.

stimulus—anything causing a response. A touch is a stimulus to touch receptors in the skin. The plural of stimulus is stimuli.

sweat glands—glands in the dermis of the skin that help cool the body by carrying water to the skin's surface.

tactile—touchable. Anything that can be detected by the sense of touch.

tendons—bands of tough tissue that connect muscles to bones.

thalamus—an area of the brain that acts as a switching station, sorting and relaying messages to other parts of the brain.

threshold of pain—the strength of a pain stimulus that must be reached in order for a person to feel the pain. People with a low pain threshold experience more pain than those who have a higher pain threshold.

vibrissae—strong, thicker-than-normal hairs commonly called whiskers. In cats, rodents, and some other mammals, vibrissae are important extensions of the sense of touch.

Index

Page numbers for illustrations are in boldface.